NATIONAL GEOGRAPHIC KiDS

LITTLE KIDS FIRST Nature Guide

BUGS

Alli Brydon

NATIONAL GEOGRAPHIC
WASHINGTON, D.C.

Table of CONTENTS

ORCHID MANTIS

JUMPING SPIDER

HORNET

The Wonderful
WORLD OF BUGS

People call a lot of creepy-crawly creatures "bugs," from butterflies and bees to spiders and worms. These animals crawl on the ground, fly in the sky, and swim in the water.

Amazing bugs are **all around,** just waiting to be **found!**

OUTDOORS

You can find creepy-crawlies on flowers, leaves, trees, and the ground, as well as in puddles and the soil.

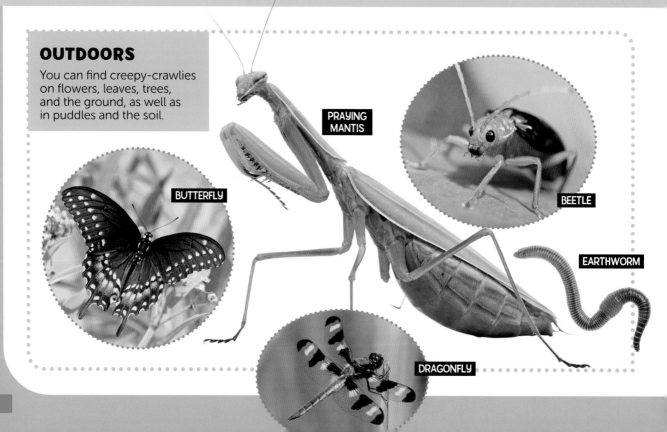

PRAYING MANTIS

BEETLE

BUTTERFLY

EARTHWORM

DRAGONFLY

CRICKET

ROLY-POLY

SPIDER

ANTS

FRUIT FLY

INDOORS

Bugs can also live inside houses. You might find them on walls, in corners, near lightbulbs, in sinks, and near your fruit bowl.

Let's Explore!

To search for bugs, use your senses. Use your eyes to look up, down, and all around. Use your ears to listen for insects buzzing or chirping. You can even use your nose to sniff for stinky bugs.

Move slowly and quietly, and don't forget to look under rocks and leaves. When you find an interesting bug, notice its shape and size and color. Watch how it moves. There are so many cool bugs to discover!

AN **ENTOMOLOGIST** IS A SCIENTIST WHO **STUDIES BUGS.**

If you find a **word you don't know,** look it up in the **glossary on page 46.**

STAY SAFE!

Be kind and careful with bugs when you are searching for them. Look with your eyes only—never touch bugs or take them from where they are resting, crawling, or flying. Some bugs sting or bite to protect themselves.

IO MOTH CATERPILLAR

WHAT TO BRING

1. A notebook and a pencil to write down or draw what you see.

2. Binoculars or a magnifying glass to help you see up close.

3. Your curiosity, a grown-up to help you explore—**and this book!**

Nice to Meet You!

Bugs are animals, and so are you! But insects and spiders don't have a backbone inside their bodies like you do. Instead they have a shell-like covering on the outside of their bodies. This covering is called an exoskeleton.

Scientists think that for every **one person, there are 200 million insects!**

TOTAL NUMBER OF INSECTS IN THE WORLD =

10,000,000,000,000,000,000

(THAT'S 10 QUINTILLION!)

BODY PARTS OF AN INSECT

All insects have six legs and three main body parts: head, thorax, and abdomen. Insects usually have wings and antennae, too.

AN INSECT USES ITS **ANTENNAE TO SMELL OR TO FEEL.**

ANTENNA

HEAD

THORAX

WING

LEG

ABDOMEN

MOST ADULT INSECTS **HAVE WINGS** AND CAN FLY.

How Do I Grow?

An insect changes a lot as it grows from a baby to an adult. There are two ways that insects grow.

WHAT DID YOU LOOK LIKE WHEN YOU WERE BORN?

Some insects, like the praying mantis, look just like their parents when they hatch. These insects go through THREE steps to become an adult:

1 EGG. A female praying mantis lays an egg sac with about 100 to 200 eggs inside.

2 NYMPH. When an egg hatches, a baby called a nymph pops out. It is very hungry and eats a lot of insects.

3 ADULT. As the nymph gets bigger, it grows new skin that fits better. Its old skin falls off. After a while, the nymph stops growing. Now it is an adult.

Some insects, such as butterflies, look very different from their parents when they hatch. These insects go through FOUR steps to become an adult:

1 EGG. A monarch butterfly lays her egg on a plant.

2 LARVA. A baby caterpillar hatches from the egg! It is now called a larva. It eats the plant it hatched on and grows bigger.

3 PUPA. When it is big enough, the caterpillar becomes a pupa. Inside the pupa, the caterpillar turns into a butterfly.

4 ADULT. After about three weeks, the butterfly comes out. Fly, butterfly!

Turn the page to **meet some more bugs!**

Super-strong Ants

Ants have superstrength. They can carry items that are a hundred times their own body weight. That would be like you carrying a car on your back!

LEAFCUTTER ANT

MY SIZE: about as long as a pencil eraser

MY COLOR: brown

MY HOME: forests and farmland in Central and South America

MY FOOD: fungus

Most ants live in large groups called colonies. Each ant in a colony has its own job. Some ants build the nest in a tree or underground. Others gather food. Each colony has a large, winged queen ant. Her only job is to lay eggs.

GREEN TREE ANT QUEEN

HOUSE ANT EGGS

HOUSE ANTS WILL **CRAWL TOWARD ANYTHING SWEET** THAT'S LEFT LYING AROUND!

FIRE ANT
Fire ants are red stinging insects. Their bite feels like burning fire!

BULLDOG ANT
Bulldog ants have knifelike jaws and a stinger in their bellies.

HOUSE ANT
These small brown ants live indoors and outdoors. They eat sugar and nectar.

Busy Bees

Buzz, buzz, buzzzzzzz! Some bees live together in colonies. A bee colony usually lives inside a hive in a tree or under the ground.

WESTERN HONEYBEE

MY SIZE: a little larger than a marble

MY COLOR: black, brown, and yellow

MY HOME: meadows, gardens, and woods; worldwide except Antarctica

MY FOOD: honey, nectar, and pollen

Bees spread pollen from plant to plant. When they land on a flower, their legs pick up pollen and carry it to the next flower. Powdery pollen helps create seeds for new flowers to grow! Some bees also make honey. They bring flower nectar back to the hive. The bees turn the nectar into honey.

BEE MAKING HONEY

POLLEN

"POLLINATE" MEANS TO **SPREAD POLLEN FROM ONE PLANT TO ANOTHER.** FLIES, MOSQUITOES, BUTTERFLIES, MOTHS, AND SOME BEETLES ARE ALSO POLLINATORS!

WILD WASPS

Like bees, wasps buzz. And some kinds of wasps look a lot like bees!

YELLOW JACKET

Yellow jackets get angry if they are disturbed and can sting many times.

PAPER WASP

A queen paper wasp builds a nest with small, chewed-up pieces of wood.

HORNET

These large wasps don't like a fight. They only sting if they think their nest is being attacked.

LADYBUG

MY SIZE: about as long as your pinkie nail

MY COLOR: many different colors and patterns, including red, orange, yellow, pink, white, and black

MY HOME: nearly every kind of habitat, worldwide except Antarctica

MY FOOD: insects, pollen, and plants

So Many Beetles

Ladybugs are beetles. There are more than 400,000 kinds of beetles. They come in many different colors, shapes, and sizes. Beetles live everywhere, except the oceans and Antarctica.

RHINOCEROS BEETLE

Ladybugs and other beetles have two pairs of wings. When the front wings are closed, they form a strong, hard covering for the beetle's body. The back wings are used for flying.

SEVEN-SPOTTED LADYBUG

GLOWING FIREFLIES

Fireflies are a special kind of beetle. They twinkle and glow on a summer night. Their bodies make their own light. Fireflies "talk" by flashing this light. Each kind of firefly has its own flashing pattern!

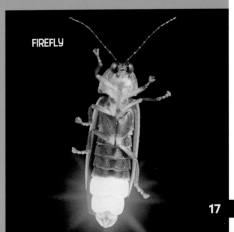

FIREFLY

RAINBOW SCARAB

Rainbow scarab is a colorful name for this North American dung beetle. Dung is poop, and that is what this beetle eats!

Meet More BEETLES

SIX-SPOTTED TIGER BEETLE

These beetles have six spots on their front wings. Count them!

JEWEL BEETLE

There are more than 15,000 kinds of jewel beetles around the world.

FIERY SEARCHER BEETLE

This is one of the largest beetles found in North America. It's about the length of your thumb!

GOLDEN TORTOISE BEETLE

This beetle can pull its legs under its shell—just like a tortoise!

VIOLIN BEETLE

These beetles are flat and shaped like leaves. This helps them camouflage, or blend in, to protect themselves.

HAVE YOU EVER SPOTTED A BEETLE?

BIGGEST & SMALLEST

The smallest beetle, *Scydosella,* can only be seen under a microscope.

SCYDOSELLA

The beetle with the longest body is the titan beetle. It grows almost as big as an adult's hand!

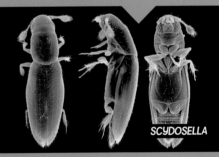

TITAN BEETLE

Beautiful Butterflies

Butterflies flutter through the air with large wings. These beautiful insects land on flowers to drink nectar.

In most places throughout the world, butterflies are out during the day. Watch them fly!

EASTERN TIGER SWALLOWTAIL

PIPEVINE SWALLOWTAIL

WHAT COLOR BUTTERFLIES HAVE YOU SEEN?

MONARCH BUTTERFLY

MY SIZE: about as wide as a playing card

MY COLOR: orange and black

MY HOME: open fields with flowers and other plants, in North America

MY FOOD: Monarch butterflies sip nectar from flowers. The caterpillars eat milkweed leaves.

BIGGEST & SMALLEST

The smallest butterfly is the western pygmy blue. Its wingspan is no bigger than the head of your toothbrush.

The largest butterfly is the Queen Alexandra's birdwing. Its wingspan can be as wide as a dinner plate!

WESTERN PYGMY BLUE

QUEEN ALEXANDRA'S BIRDWING

Marvelous Moths

Moths have big wings, just like butterflies. It can be hard to tell these two insects apart.

CHECK ME OUT! LUNA MOTH

MY SIZE: as wide as a playing card

MY COLOR: green, yellow, and blue

MY HOME: forests in North America

MY FOOD: Caterpillars eat leaves from hickory, walnut, sumac, and persimmon trees.

Here's how to spot the difference between moths and butterflies:

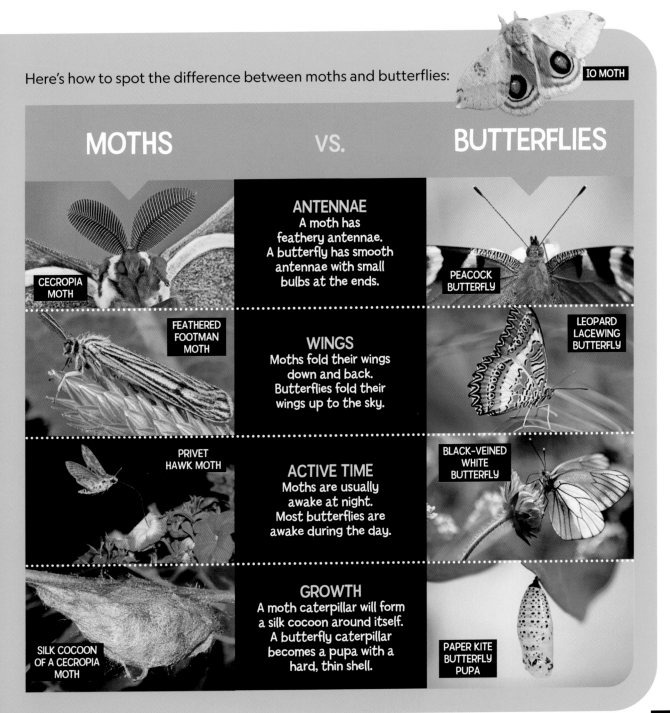

IO MOTH

MOTHS VS. BUTTERFLIES

CECROPIA MOTH

ANTENNAE
A moth has feathery antennae. A butterfly has smooth antennae with small bulbs at the ends.

PEACOCK BUTTERFLY

FEATHERED FOOTMAN MOTH

WINGS
Moths fold their wings down and back. Butterflies fold their wings up to the sky.

LEOPARD LACEWING BUTTERFLY

PRIVET HAWK MOTH

ACTIVE TIME
Moths are usually awake at night. Most butterflies are awake during the day.

BLACK-VEINED WHITE BUTTERFLY

SILK COCOON OF A CECROPIA MOTH

GROWTH
A moth caterpillar will form a silk cocoon around itself. A butterfly caterpillar becomes a pupa with a hard, thin shell.

PAPER KITE BUTTERFLY PUPA

Fly, Dragonflies!

A dragonfly has four wings that flap very fast. They help the dragonfly move forward, backward, and side to side. These wings also help it turn quickly and even hang in the air like a helicopter!

SOMBRE GOLDENRING

GREEN-EYED HAWKER

CHECK ME OUT! COMMON GREEN DARNER

MY SIZE: about as long as a playing card

MY COLOR: green and brown

MY HOME: ponds and wetlands, mainly in North and Central America

MY FOOD: mosquitoes and other insects

A DRAGONFLY **USES ITS LEGS TO GRAB SMALL INSECTS** TO EAT— SOMETIMES EVEN WHILE FLYING!

MEET MORE
DRAGONFLIES

WHICH DRAGONFLY IS YOUR FAVORITE?

SOUTHERN HAWKER

This is one of the largest and fastest dragonflies in the world!

FEMALE KIRBY'S DROPWING

KIRBY'S DROPWING SKIMMER

This dragonfly comes in two bright colors: The females are yellow, and the males are red.

FLAG-TAILED SPINYLEG

This dragonfly has spikes on its legs. It uses these spikes to catch a meal.

MALE KIRBY'S DROPWING

HALLOWEEN PENNANT

This dragonfly is orange and black. Most dragonflies hide in wind or rain, but these don't.

Chirping Crickets

On warm summer nights, male crickets chirp loudly by rubbing their front wings together. Chirps are how they "talk" to female crickets. Female crickets do not chirp at all. But both male and female crickets have very good hearing.

SNOWY TREE CRICKET

MY SIZE: about the size of a kidney bean

MY COLOR: green, orange, and black

MY HOME: shrubs, vines, and trees throughout most of the United States

MY FOOD: aphids, small insects, grass, and fungus

Go, Grasshoppers!

Grasshoppers and crickets are related. Both have four wings for flying and large hind legs for jumping. And both are very noisy! But grasshoppers have shorter antennae, are active during the day, and eat only plants.

BLUE-WINGED GRASSHOPPER

LUBBER GRASSHOPPERS **MAKE A HISSING NOISE** TO SCARE OFF ENEMIES.

CHECK ME OUT!

EASTERN LUBBER GRASSHOPPER

MY SIZE: about as long as a playing card

MY COLOR: orange, yellow, red, and black

MY HOME: grass, fields, and woods in the southern United States

MY FOOD: grass, weeds, and leaves

Super Cicadas

These large insects are noisy. The male cicada has a special body part on its belly. It's called a tymbal. It makes loud buzzing and clicking sounds.

CHECK ME OUT!

PERIODICAL CICADA

MY SIZE: about the size of your pinkie finger

MY COLOR: black and orange

MY HOME: underground and in trees and shrubs in parts of the United States

MY FOOD: tree sap

DOG DAY CICADA

Cicadas come out during the summertime to eat and lay eggs. As cicadas grow bigger, they leave their skin behind on tree trunks. This is called molting.

HIDDEN CICADAS

This is the 17-year cicada. The females lay their eggs in tree branches. When the eggs hatch, the cicada nymphs drop and bury themselves underground. They live there for 17 years, growing and molting. Then the nymphs leave the ground and crawl up tree trunks. They molt one last time to become adults.

17-YEAR PERIODICAL CICADA

CHECK ME OUT! PRAYING MANTIS

MY SIZE: about as long as a small lemon

MY COLOR: green

MY HOME: trees, meadows, and gardens throughout most of the world

MY FOOD: insects

Sneaky Praying Mantises

A praying mantis sits very still. It blends in with grass or leaves. Then, SNATCH! Its legs shoot out and grab a buggy meal.

A mantis might look like it is praying, with its front legs bent and folded together. But it is really looking for its next prey.

MEET MORE MANTISES

CONEHEAD MANTIS

This mantis looks like it's wearing a cone-shaped hat!

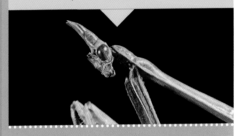

MALAYSIAN ORCHID MANTIS

This mantis looks like an orchid to blend in with flowers.

SPINY FLOWER MANTIS

This mantis can scare off predators. It spreads its wings to show giant eyespot markings.

31

Terrific Treehoppers

There are more than 3,500 kinds of treehoppers. They come in many different colors and shapes. Some look like they have horns, thorns, or leaves on their backs.

CHECK ME OUT! THORN MIMIC TREEHOPPER

MY SIZE: about the size of a blueberry

MY COLOR: a variety of colors

MY HOME: mostly in tropical forests; on all continents except Antarctica

MY FOOD: the sap from plants

Treehoppers and ants help each other. Treehoppers drink sap from plants. Then they let out a sweet liquid called honeydew. Ants drink the honeydew off the treehoppers. As the ants drink, they surround the treehoppers and protect them.

HOW DO YOU HELP OTHERS?

OAK TREEHOPPERS **HANG OUT IN GROUPS.** YOU CAN OFTEN FIND 50 TO 100 OF THEM TOGETHER.

ANT-MIMICKING TREEHOPPER
This treehopper looks like it has an ant on its back.

OAK TREEHOPPER
This treehopper often has a horn that sticks out from its head.

CLADONOTA BENITEZI
What does this treehopper look like to you?

33

Surprising Stick Insects

A stick insect looks like a stick. It's hard to see on a tree. This insect's color, shape, and size help it blend in. That helps it hide from hungry predators.

CHECK ME OUT! CHAN'S MEGASTICK

MY SIZE: about the size of an adult's arm

MY COLOR: brown

MY HOME: rainforests on Borneo, a large island in Asia

MY FOOD: leaves

The common walking stick and the giant walking stick can both be found in North America. When a predator is nearby, these insects sit still. They tuck their legs close to their bodies. This helps them look like a stick!

COMMON WALKING STICK INSECT

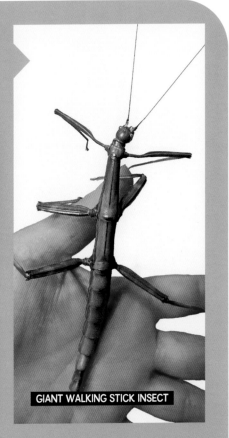

GIANT WALKING STICK INSECT

IF YOU COULD LOOK LIKE SOMETHING ELSE, WHAT WOULD IT BE?

UNBE-LEAF-ABLE

Stick insects aren't the only bugs that blend in with trees. This insect from Asia looks like a leaf! Can you find its head and legs?

LEAF INSECT

Stinky Stink Bugs

HAVE YOU EVER SMELLED A STINK BUG'S STINK?

BROWN MARMORATED STINK BUG

When a stink bug is in danger, it sprays a stinky liquid. Then it beats its wings to spread the smell. This tells predators, "Stay away from me! I taste bad!"

IT'S TRUE!

Stink bugs are known as "true bugs." Other true bugs are treehoppers and cicadas. What are true bugs?

They grow from an egg to a nymph to an adult, like this large milkweed bug.

They have sharp, sucking mouthparts, like this kissing bug. *Mwah!*

Their back wings are usually see-through and stay tucked underneath the front wings, like with this shield bug.

COMMON GREEN SHIELD BUG

THIS STINK BUG **HARMS FARMERS' CROPS.**

A Spider's World

SPINY ORB WEAVER

GREEN CRAB SPIDER

Spiders are not insects. They are a kind of animal called arachnids. Spiders have two main body parts: head and abdomen. They have eight legs.

GOLDENROD CRAB SPIDER

THIS SPIDER HAS **TRAPPED AN INSECT** IN ITS WEB.

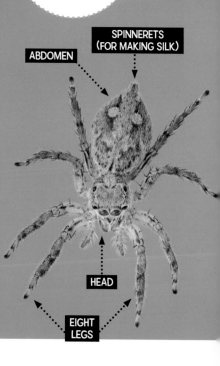

ABDOMEN

SPINNERETS (FOR MAKING SILK)

HEAD

EIGHT LEGS

CHECK ME OUT!

HOUSE SPIDER

MY SIZE: about the size of a penny

MY COLOR: brown and beige

MY HOME: houses worldwide

MY FOOD: insects

WHAT A WEB

Most spiders build webs out of silk. They make silk inside their bodies in a special place called spinnerets. A spiderweb is sticky. When an insect flies into the web, it cannot get out. Now the spider has a tasty meal. Here are a few kinds of spiderwebs:

FUNNEL WEB
Funnel-web spiders spin webs that look like a tunnel.

SHEET WEB
Sheet-weaver spiders spin a web that looks like a flat sheet on top of bushes.

SPIRAL WEB
The orb-weaver spider spins a flat, round web.

WHEEL SPIDER

This spider cartwheels down sand dunes to escape from predators.

Meet More SPIDERS

JUMPING SPIDER

There are about 5,000 kinds of spiders that jump. *Boing!*

GOLIATH BIRD-EATING TARANTULA

The Goliath bird-eating tarantula is the biggest spider in the world. It could cover a whole dinner plate!

PEACOCK SPIDER

The male peacock spider does a dance to attract a female.

BIRD-DROPPING SPIDER

This spider looks like poop to keep predators away.

A SPIDER'S LIFE

A spider's life has three stages. Below is the life cycle of an orb weaver:

1 A female spider lays an egg sac with a thousand eggs inside.

2 Tiny baby spiders, called spiderlings, hatch from the eggs.

3 After a few months, the spiderlings grow into adults and go off on their own.

TRAPDOOR SPIDER

This spider hides inside a hole and covers it with a "trapdoor" made of dirt and silk. Then it pops out to catch an insect for its meal.

THERE ARE **MORE THAN 45,000 KINDS** OF SPIDERS!

Earthworms
Dig Dirt

Earthworms crawl through dirt in gardens and fields. They eat the dirt and then poop it out. This helps make the dirt a good place for plants to grow.

Most of the time, earthworms stay underground. But they do come up to the surface sometimes.

CHECK ME OUT!

EARTHWORM

MY SIZE: usually only about as long as your pointer finger, but they can grow longer than a pencil

MY COLOR: brown and beige

MY HOME: under the soil in North America, Asia, and Europe

MY FOOD: plants in the soil

EARTHWORMS ARE SHAPED LIKE TUBES. **THEY ARE NOT INSECTS.**

Roly-Poly Pillbugs

These little bugs can roll up into a ball. That's why they are also called roly-polies. Pillbugs like to hide under rocks and stones.

PILLBUG

MY SIZE: about the size of a pea

MY COLOR: dark gray

MY HOME: under the ground or under rocks in North America and Europe

MY FOOD: rotting plants and animals

Pillbugs eat plants and animals that are dead and rotting. This helps clean up the outdoors!

PILLBUGS ARE NOT INSECTS. THEY ARE CRUSTACEANS. THIS MEANS THEY ARE RELATED TO CRABS AND SHRIMP.

ROLLED UP

UNROLLING

UNROLLED AND READY TO FLIP OVER

43

HIDE-AND-SEEK!

Can you find these hard-to-spot bugs?

LEAF INSECT

WALKING STICK

LOBSTER MOTH

PILLBUG

Answers on page 48.

MOVE LIKE A BUG!

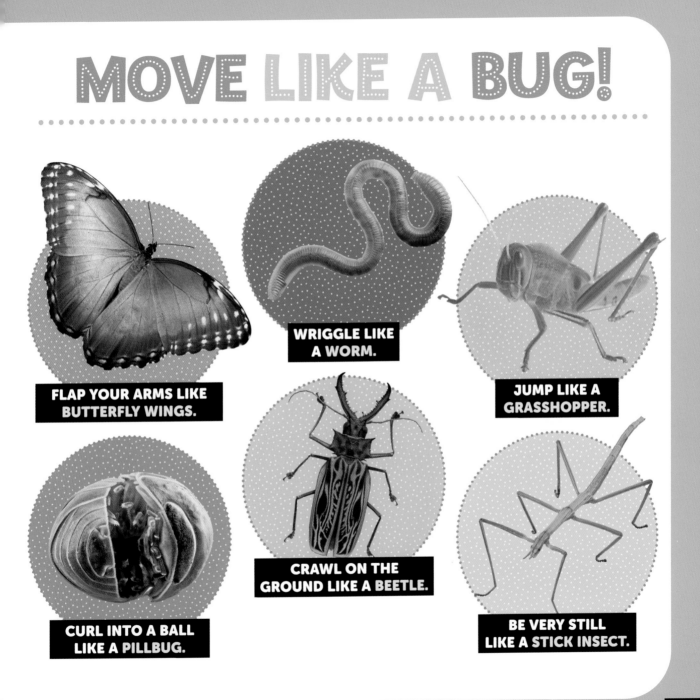

FLAP YOUR ARMS LIKE BUTTERFLY WINGS.

WRIGGLE LIKE A WORM.

JUMP LIKE A GRASSHOPPER.

CURL INTO A BALL LIKE A PILLBUG.

CRAWL ON THE GROUND LIKE A BEETLE.

BE VERY STILL LIKE A STICK INSECT.

GLOSSARY

ABDOMEN A bug's rear body segment.

ANTENNAE Feelers that stick out of a bug's head; they are used to feel or smell.

ARACHNID A group of animals with no backbone or antennae. They have an exoskeleton, two body regions, and usually eight legs.

CAMOUFLAGE The ability of an animal to blend in with its surroundings.

COCOON A covering that some insects, like moths, make to protect themselves as they grow into adults.

COLONY A group of bugs that live together.

CRUSTACEAN A group of mostly sea creatures that have an exoskeleton, like crabs or shrimp.

ENTOMOLOGIST A scientist who studies bugs.

EXOSKELETON A shell-like covering on the outside of a bug's body.

HONEYDEW A sugary, sticky liquid that some bugs let out as they feed on plant sap.

LARVA The young form of an insect.

MIMIC To look like something else.

MOLTING Shedding skin during growth.

NECTAR A sweet liquid that flowers make.

NYMPH A young insect.

POLLEN Dusty material at the center of a plant that helps make that plant's seeds.

POLLINATE To move pollen from place to place.

PREDATOR An animal that hunts other animals (prey) for food.

PREY An animal that a predator hunts for food.

PUPA A stage in the life of an insect when a larva becomes an adult.

SPINNERETS A spider's silk-making organ.

THORAX A bug's middle body segment with legs and wings.

INDEX

Photo
Credits

AD: Adobe Stock; AL: Alamy Stock Photo; DR: Dreamstime; GI: Getty Images; IS: iStockphoto; MP: Minden Pictures; SC: Science Source; SS: Shutterstock
Cover (green damselfly), Subbotina Anna/SS; (butterfly), James Laurie/SS; (blue damselfly face), Miroslav Hlavko/SS; (ladybug), irin-k/SS; (inchworm), BrightSpace/SS; (wasp), Kletr/SS; (spider), Eric Isselée/SS; Spine (ladybug), irin-k/SS; Back cover (UP LE), Anton Kozyrev/IS/GI; (UP RT), Theodore P. Webb/SS; (LO), Tyler Fox/SS; 1, fajrulisme/AD; 2, Kryvenok Anastasiia/SS; 3 (LE), Kurit afshen/SS; 3 (CTR), Marek Velechovsky/SS; 3 (RT), Kletr/SS; 4 (dragonfly), Paul Reeves Photo/SS; 4 (orange beetle), KozyrevAnton/IS; 4 (earthworm), nantonov/IS; 4 (green beetle), seanjoh/IS; 4 (praying mantis), Ziva_K/IS; 4 (butterfly), Brian E Kushner/AD; 4 (ladybug), irin-k/SS; 4 (inchworm), BrightSpace/SS; 4 (wasp), Kletr/SS; 5 (fruit fly), Michael Durham/MP; 5 (spider), Rob_Ellis/IS; 5 (house cricket), arisara1978/IS; 5 (ants), Jason Johnstone/AL; 5 (roly-poly), lauriek/IS; 6 (moth), Fyle/AD; 6 (fly), Denis Vesely/SS; 6 (butterfly), Lukas Gojda/SS; 6 (caterpillar), Weber/IS; 7 (UP LE), hatchapong/AD; 7 (LO LE), Amorn Suriyan/SS; 7 (RT), amelie/AD; 8 (UP), asharkyu/SS; 8 (LO), Zsschreiner/SS; 9, Pavol Klimek/AD; 10 (UP LE), eleonimages/AD; 10 (UP RT), Inzyx/IS; 10 (LO LE), Tatiana/AD; 10 (LO RT), up close with nature/GI; 11 (UP LE), MetaCynth/SS; 11 (UP CTR), Brett/AD; 11 (UP RT), Dossy/AD; 11 (LO LE), Butterfly Hunter/SS; 11 (LO CTR), Georgi Baird/SS; 11 (LO RT), Butterfly Hunter/SS; 12, Ingo Arndt/MP; 13 (UP LE), Bayu Nuse/DR; 13 (UP RT), finchfocus/SS; 13 (CTR), Johan Larson/AD; 13 (LO LE), Kenneth H. Thomas/SC; 13 (LO CTR), motazkattan/GI; 13 (LO RT), Joel Sartore/National Geographic Image Collection; 14 (CTR), Protasov AN/SS; 14 (UP RT), irin-k/SS; 14 (UP LE), Alle/DR; 15 (UP LE), Grafissimo/IS; 15 (UP CTR), formplus/AD; 15 (UP RT), Tsekhmister/SS; 15 (LO LE), Randall Runtsch/SS; 15 (LO CTR), SimplyCreativePhotography/IS; 15 (LO RT), TTstudio/AD; 16, Mironmax Studio/SS; 17 (UP), Mark Brandon/SS; 17 (horned beetle), Dja65/SS; 17 (black beetle), irin-k/SS; 17 (green beetle), Tea Maeklong/SS; 17 (LO LE), Joel Heras/MindenPictures; 17 (LO RT), Cathy Keifer/SS; 18 (UP), George Grall/AL; 18 (LO LE), Chanachola/SS; 18 (LO RT), Digital Images Studio/SS; 19 (UP LE), pimmimemom/AD; 19 (UP RT), yusuf kurnia/SS; 19 (LO LE), Vince Adam/SS; 19 (CTR RT), Alexey Polivov; 19 (LO RT), Margus Vilbas/SS; 20 (UP ALL), Lukas Gojda/SS; 20 (LO LE), Steve Satushek/GI; 20 (LO RT), Sari ONeal/SS; 21 (UP), Sari ONeal/SS; 21 (LO LE), Naturekind/DR; 21 (LO RT), DEEPU SG/AL; 22, David Havel/SS; 23 (UP), Mirror-Images/SS; 23 (Up A), Cathy Keifer/SS; 23 (Up B), DmyTo/AD; 23 (Up C), Eduardo Dzphoto/SS; 23 (Up D), Leena Robinson/SS; 23 (Lo E), Ysign/SS; 23 (Lo F), Marek Mierzejewski/SS; 23 (Lo G), Matt Jeppson/SS; 23 (Lo H), MilletStudio/SS; 24 (UP), Eric Isselée/SS; 24 (CTR), alisluch/AD; 24 (LO), Paul Reeves/DR; 25 (UP LE), Naturfoto Honal/GI; 25 (UP RT), Biosphoto/AL; 25 (LO LE), Bryan Reynolds/AL; 25 (LO CTR), Jim Schwabel/AD; 25 (LO RT), Simon_g/SS; 26 (UP), Scott Camazine/SC; 26 (LO), John W. Bova/SC; 27 (UP), Dietmar Nill/MP; 27 (LO), Tyler Fox/SS; 28 (UP), zcy/AD; 28 (LO), Mary Terriberry/SS; 29 (UP LE), chas53/AD; 29 (UP RT), Jamie Noguchi/SS; 29 (LO), Joe Austin Photography/AL; 30, Alberto Ghizzi Panizza/MP; 31 (UP), zagursky/AD; 31 (CTR), Kuritafsheen/DR; 31 (LO LE), Cam/AD; 31 (LO RT), SemilirBanyu/AD; 32, salparadis/AD; 33 (UP LE), Pavel Krasensky/SS; 33 (UP RT), Premaphotos/Nature Picture LIbrary; 33 (UP), Clarence Holmes Wildlife/AL; 33 (LO LE), Clarence Holmes Wildlife/AL; 33 (LO RT), Patrick Landmann/SC; 34 (UP), Sigit Kurniawan/SS; 34 (LO), Chuck Holliday; 35 (UP LE), Brian Lasenby/AD; 35 (UP RT), Macstock/DR; 35 (LO), PeingjaiChiangmai/SS; 36, Chinahbzyx/DR; 37 (UP LE), Melinda Fawver/AD; 37 (UP RT), photobee/AD; 37 (UP CTR RT), drsuth48/SS; 37 (LO CTR RT), Tuty Farida/DR; 37 (LO LE), Radu Bercan/SS; 37 (LO RT), Westend61/GI; 38 (UP LE), T3rmiit/DR; 38 (UP CTR), Henrik Larsson/SS; 38 (UP RT), Paul Wolf/AD; 38 (LO LE), andrewbalcombe/AD; 38 (LO RT), AjayTvm/SS; 39 (UP), boyphare/SS; 39 (LO LE), Wakhron/AD; 39 (LO RT), Mikel Bilbao Gorostiaga-Nature & Landscapes/AL; 40 (UP LE), Michael and Patricia Fogden/MP; 40 (UP RT), Biosphoto/AL; 40 (LO LE), Stephen Dalton/MP; 40 (LO RT), Audrey Snider-Bell/SS; 41 (UP LE), Ruzy Hartini/SS; 41 (CTR RT), WAHLBRINK-Photo/SS; 41 (UP RT), Rod Hill/IS; 41 (LO LE), Ken Griffiths/SS; 41 (LO RT), Kirill Burtasovs/SS; 42 (UP LE), Valentina Razumova/SS; 42 (UP RT), D. Kucharski K. Kucharska/SS; 42 (LO), Heidi and Hans-Juergen Koch/MP; 43 (UP LE), paulrommer/AD; 43 (UP CTR), Stuart Hamilton/SS; 43 (UP RT), DBA/AD; 43 (LO ALL), Kubo Hidekazu/MP; 44 (UP LE), Akkharat Jarusilawong/SS; 44 (UP RT), KarSol/SS; 44 (LO LE), Ian Redding/SS; 44 (LO RT), Theresa White/SS; 45 (UP LE), Milous Chab/DR; 45 (UP CTR), Valentina Razumova/SS; 45 (UP RT), nednapa/SS; 45 (LO LE), Cristina Romero Palma/SS; 45 (LO CTR), Dja65/SS; 45 (LO RT), Cristina Romero Palma/SS; 46 (UP), nantonov/IS; 46 (LO LE), KozyrevAnton/IS; 46 (LO CTR), BrightSpace/SS; 46 (LO RT), Lukas Gojda/SS; 47 (UP), Henrik Larsson/SS; 47 (LO), Tea Maeklong/SS

For Rhys and his roly-poly pet, Arthur —A. B.

Published by National Geographic Partners, LLC, Washington, DC 20036.

Designed by Sanjida Rashid

The publisher gratefully acknowledges entomologist Dr. William O. Lamp of the University of Maryland for his expert review of this book, and Dr. Tovah P. Klein, director of the Barnard College Center for Toddler Development, for her advice and expertise. Many thanks also to project manager Grace Hill Smith, photo editor Sharon Dortenzio, and researcher Jennifer Geddes for their invaluable help with this project.

Library of Congress Cataloging-in-Publication Data

Names: Brydon, Alli, author.
Title: Bugs / Alli Brydon.
Description: Washington, D.C. : National Geographic Kids, 2022. I Series: Little kids first nature guide I Includes index. I Audience: Ages 4-8 I Audience: Grades 2-3 I
Identifiers: LCCN 2020005734 I ISBN 9781426371493 (hardcover) I ISBN 9781426371509 (library binding)
Subjects: LCSH: Hemiptera--Juvenile literature. I Insects--Juvenile literature.
Classification: LCC QL521 .B84 2022 I DDC 595.7/54--dc23
LC record available at https://lccn.loc.gov/2020005734

Printed in China
22/RRDH/1